The Expert's Guide on

How to Sell a House in the UK:

helping you to sell well.

by

Dr Judith Summer
of
Simma Properties

Simma Properties - Finding your little property treasure
Copyright © 2016 Judith Penina Summer
All rights reserved.

**The Expert's Guide on How to Sell a House in the UK:
helping you to sell well.
by Dr Judith Summer.**

Copyright and Disclaimer

All rights reserved. No part of this publication may be reproduced, stored in a retrieval system, or transmitted, in any form or by any means electronic, mechanical, photocopying, recording or otherwise, without the prior written permission of Judith Penina Summer.

I can be contacted via my website at http://www.simmaproperties.co.uk

Whilst every effort has been made to ensure that the information contained in this book is correct, the author cannot accept any responsibility for any errors or omissions or for any consequences resulting therefrom.

Whilst I hope to be able to help you, I cannot be held responsible or liable in contract or in tort or in any way if there are any inaccuracies in this book and/or if my advice does not work for you and/or your circumstances. All I can say is that my approach works for me and has helped me to build a successful property portfolio. I hope it may guide you in similar successes, although of course there is no guarantee. This book does not contain tailored advice for your particular circumstances and I do not pretend to know what the market conditions in your area are like either now or in the future. Please do not construe any advice given in this book as a command or a rule or a statement of fact. My advice is mere guidance to be adapted by you as necessary in all the circumstances of the case, and it reflects my opinions. The opinions I express are my own, and you may well disagree with them. Remember that buying and selling property is more of an art than a science, and there are no formulae or hard and fast rules as to what works best in any particular circumstance. You must not rely on information in this book as an alternative to legal or other qualified professional advice. This disclaimer will be governed by and construed in accordance with English law, and any disputes relating to this disclaimer will be subject to the exclusive jurisdiction of the courts of England and Wales.

Simma Properties - Finding your little property treasure
Copyright © 2016 Judith Penina Summer
All rights reserved.

Simma Properties - Finding your little property treasure
Copyright © 2016 Judith Penina Summer
All rights reserved.

**The Expert's Guide on How to Sell a House in the UK: helping you to sell well.
by Dr Judith Summer.**

Blurb

In 8 easy readable chapters, this book covers how to prepare you home, whether it is a house or a flat, to put it into optimum sale condition. The aim is for the seller to try to maximise the potential sale value and not lose out on potential buyers. This book should empower the seller to choose the right estate agent, value the property and understand and manage the sale process. Each chapter concludes with a summary of top tips.

There is a sister book written by me: The Expert's Guide on How to Buy a House in the UK: helping you to buy a good home and a good property investment. This can also be found on Amazon. I have made an effort not to duplicate the information in each book.

Further books may follow!

In the meantime, my blog and property finding services can be accessed via my website: http://www.simmaproperties.co.uk/index.php and you can find my TV interviews for Sky's Property Panorama on my YouTube Channel (Judith Summer at Simma Properties).

Enjoy!

Simma Properties - Finding your little property treasure
Copyright © 2016 Judith Penina Summer
All rights reserved.

The Expert's Guide on How to Sell a House in the UK: helping you to sell well.
by Dr Judith Summer.

Contents

Introduction
   Overview
   How do I know what I am talking about?
   This book and its sister book
Chapter 1
Declutter your home
   1.1   Living rooms
   1.2   Papers and books.
   1.3   Kitchen
   1.4   Bedrooms
   1.5   Hallways
   1.6   Bathrooms
   1.7   A boxroom
   1.8   People who can help you declutter, charities and sale of goods.
   1.9   Make the time to declutter
   1.10   Summary top tips
Chapter 2
Floors, furnishings and smells
   2.1   Wood floors
   2.2   Rugs and carpets
   2.3   Flowery, lacy or frilly soft furnishings
   2.4   Colours
   2.5   Beds
   2.6   Curtains
   2.7   Dressing the property for sale
   2.8   Smells
   2.9   Summary top tips
Chapter 3
Repairs and renovations
   3.1   Repairs
   3.2   Painting
   3.3   When a property clearly needs renovation
   3.4   Summary top tips
Chapter 4

Simma Properties - Finding your little property treasure
Copyright © 2016 Judith Penina Summer
All rights reserved.

The Expert's Guide on How to Sell a House in the UK: helping you to sell well.
by Dr Judith Summer.

Preparing the outside for sale
- 4.1 Front and back gardens
- 4.2 Big trees and overhanging foliage
- 4.3 Fences
- 4.4 Bins
- 4.5 Front door
- 4.6 Window frames and sills
- 4.7 Guttering and hoppers
- 4.8 Summary top tips

Chapter 5

Appointing an estate agent
- 5.1 Do you need an estate agent?
- 5.2 "Online" estate agents
- 5.3 The value that an estate agent adds to the process
- 5.4 What if someone approaches you for a private sale?
- 5.5 How do you appoint the right estate agent?
- 5.6 How many estate agents should you appoint?
- 5.7 Summary top tips

Chapter 6

Preparing your property for a viewing
- 6.1 Clean and tidy
- 6.2 Beds
- 6.3 Flowers
- 6.4 Garden
- 6.5 Light
- 6.6 Temperature
- 6.7 Pets
- 6.8 People out of the way
- 6.9 Smells
- 6.10 Checklist
- 6.11 What if you only have half an hour's notice before a viewing?
- 6.12 Summary top tips

Chapter 7

Preparing for the sale process
- 7.1 Appoint a solicitor
- 7.2 Documents
- 7.3 Removal company

Simma Properties - Finding your little property treasure
Copyright © 2016 Judith Penina Summer
All rights reserved.

The Expert's Guide on How to Sell a House in the UK: helping you to sell well.
by Dr Judith Summer.

    7.4   Mental preparation
    7.5   Do you have somewhere to move to?
    7.6   Obtaining the local searches
    7.7   Summary top tips

Chapter 8

The Sale Process (for England and Wales)
    8.1   Offer, exchange, completion
    8.2   Timing between offer, acceptance and completion
    8.3   Gazumping (a new buyer coming along with a higher offer)
    8.4   Lock out agreements
    8.5   What if the buyer drops his offer?
    8.6   Between exchange and completion
    8.7   After completion
    8.8   Summary top tips

Epilogue

Simma Properties - Finding your little property treasure
Copyright © 2016 Judith Penina Summer
All rights reserved.

The Expert's Guide on How to Sell a House in the UK: helping you to sell well.
by **Dr Judith Summer.**

Simma Properties - Finding your little property treasure
Copyright © 2016 Judith Penina Summer
All rights reserved.

The Expert's Guide on How to Sell a House in the UK:
helping you to sell well.
by Dr Judith Summer.

Introduction

Overview

How do I know what I am talking about?

This book and its sister book

Overview

The UK is experiencing high property prices and fierce competition in the residential market as demand for housing continues to far outweigh supply. The results of the referendum for the UK to leave the EU do not change this. In this book I aim to help sellers navigate the challenges of achieving a good and smooth sale of their home.

This book should help sellers in the UK from all walks of life, whether they have much or little experience of selling property and whether they are selling a small flat or a large house. It is based on the accumulation of my experience in a strong and vibrant market. I will give general advice which will apply nationally like how to get your home ready for sale, but I will also give an overview of the legal system for conveyancing particular to England and Wales.

How do I know what I am talking about?

Trust me, I'm a lawyer! Actually I am a non-practising solicitor with a Cambridge degree in law and a PhD in law.

But I also have nearly a decade of experience in investing in the property market of a prime residential area of central London. I have learnt to spot and buy a bargain for my own portfolio. I have more than once sold my own property so as to achieve the highest price per square foot on the particular road.

Simma Properties - Finding your little property treasure
Copyright © 2016 Judith Penina Summer
All rights reserved.

**The Expert's Guide on How to Sell a House in the UK:
helping you to sell well.
by Dr Judith Summer.**

I founded Simma Properties and now also act as a property finder and development consultant, spreading my expertise as far as I can. It may interest you to follow my twitter account @simmaproperties where I tweet about current UK property market news and trends. I have also appeared on Sky television giving property advice. . I write a property blog via tumblr which can be found at: http://www.tumblr.com/blog/judithsummer
or
http://www.simmaproperties.co.uk/blog.php

This book and its sister book

This book is about selling a home in the UK. I have tried to include everything that I think is relevant, although of course there may be some things that I have not thought to add.

There is also a separate sister book about buying a home in the UK. But it will help a seller to know what a buyer should be doing, and it will help a buyer to know what a seller should be doing, so feel free to read both books! I have aimed to make it so that information contained in one book is not repeated in the other.

Simma Properties - Finding your little property treasure
Copyright © 2016 Judith Penina Summer
All rights reserved.

The Expert's Guide on How to Sell a House in the UK:
helping you to sell well.
by Dr Judith Summer.

Chapter 1

Declutter your home

1.1   Living rooms

1.2   Papers and books

1.3   Kitchen

1.4   Bedrooms

1.5   Hallways

1.6   Bathrooms

1.7   A boxroom

1.8   People who can help you declutter, charities and sale of goods

1.9   Make the time to declutter

1.10 Summary top tips

There are three main steps to selling a property successfully: 1) preparing the property; 2) appointing estate agents and 3) getting the conveyancing team lined up. Decluttering your home is one of the hardest and most important steps to take in the first stage of preparing the property for sale.

**The Expert's Guide on How to Sell a House in the UK:
helping you to sell well.
by Dr Judith Summer.**

By telling you to declutter, I do not mean just put things in piles. I mean remove almost everything from sight. Clear <u>all</u> surfaces so they have one or no things on them. You may have to throw things out or put them into temporary storage, but it will make a big difference to the sale if things are clear. Even if it does not increase the sale price, it will make the place more attractive and therefore easier to sell and will not decrease the price achievable. I have seen properties stuck on the market for a long and frustrating time because the viewers could not see past the mess of the inside to understand how spacious and well-appointed the rooms were.

1.1   Living rooms

Your family photos may mean a lot to you, but the viewer is not interested in how cute your gorgeous grandchildren look, and would rather see a clear mantelpiece. Anything on show should be because it has carefully been placed to be on show. So the bright vase of flowers in the centre of a table, or the two candlesticks at either end of a mantelpiece over which a painting or mirror has been hung are all fine. The pile of old magazines sitting there because there is nowhere else to put them is not OK. That is what recycling bags are for! All little trinkets and bits of things need to be put away; the viewer does not care that you went to Margate and picked up such a lovely little thing! I repeat the mantra: try to clear all the surfaces.

1.2   Papers and books.

Papers should be filed and put away and old papers scanned if necessary and thrown out. You are not obliged to keep UK tax papers or their supporting documents for more than 7 full tax years. In fact you are not even required to keep them for that long, so why are you still storing bank statements from 1995?

Do you need all those books lined two deep on the shelves? Are you going to read any of them again? Are you sure there is no-one else in the world who might benefit from being able to read your old books? Perhaps you could give some to family members or a charity shop? Any remaining books on shelves should be lined up at the front edge of the shelf so they look neat.

**The Expert's Guide on How to Sell a House in the UK:
helping you to sell well.
by Dr Judith Summer.**

1.3   Kitchen

The more clutter you have in the kitchen, the more it shows that the kitchen is too small for the house. The top of the microwave is not a filing shelf! Put everything you possibly can in a cupboard. Any gadget not used daily should go away too if it can. Think carefully about what you can throw or give away or store. Do you really need that old set of Turkish coffee cups that Great Aunt Maud bought you once and are you ever going to use that inherited set of crockery?

1.4   Bedrooms

A bedroom should look inviting, especially the master. That means there should be no clothes in sight, there should be a clear path around the bed and bedside tables should be clear but for a few essentials - something like a book, a lamp and a box of tissues, but very little or nothing else. Wardrobes should be closed with nothing hanging on the outside. A dressing table should be clear. My husband has a strict rule - if he has not worn something for a year, it should be given away. He has a point, but I would make it a two year rule! Everyday shoes that are not comfortable are never going to be worn, so get rid of them. They will fit someone else better.

1.5   Hallways

Hallways should be clear. This is especially important at the entrance to the property, as it is the first thing that the viewer will see inside the front door. If your hallway by the front door does not have a cupboard and there is room, I would suggest a quick trip to Ikea! In that cupboard there should be space for coats, hats, scarves, gloves, shoes, umbrellas and everything else that often litters a hallway. If there is really no room for a cupboard, then at least line shoes up in a neat row, rather than thrown in a pile, and see if anything can go out of the hallway and into a wardrobe elsewhere. See if there is room for a coat stand or some hooks on the wall for coats and keys etc and perhaps an umbrella stand. If there is a console table or window ledge in the hallway, make sure it is not filled sky high with post. Installing a mirror on a hallway wall can help give a feeling of space and light.

**The Expert's Guide on How to Sell a House in the UK:
helping you to sell well.
by Dr Judith Summer.**

1.6 Bathrooms

Bathrooms should look uncluttered too. Try to put away as many tubes of ointments etc as you can, so that there is nothing much more than a toothbrush and soap in sight. If you need another bathroom cabinet, see if there is room for one. See if you can throw away old tubes of things you have not used for years. You can buy inexpensive but shiny, clean-looking, free-standing and matching toothbrush holders and soap holders in simple silver metal which usually look quite smart. Children's bath toys can be put together and if they cannot be stored out of sight, they can be put in an inexpensive net bought for the purpose and hanging from the bath tap. If the children are actually too old for the bath toys, then please throw them out!

1.7 A boxroom

Although I would not recommend this option, if you are really struggling to clear your house and you cannot afford off-site storage, it may be an option to use your smallest and least used room for storage. It may give a better impression to have one messy, cluttered room than to have mess spread throughout the property. The downside is that the viewer will have to assess your property without being able to fathom the full potential of your boxroom. If there is a bed in this room, perhaps it would look better if the things were stored under and on top of it so that the viewer could still get around the room and envisage the bed space. Do not cover the window area: maximum light will be important. If you go down this route, and I would really recommend that you try not to, it would be better if your goods were stored in boxes rather than just in one big mess, so at least the eye would see some sort of uniformity and order. Having a boxroom filled as a dumping room highlights to a viewer that there may not be enough storage space in the current property. It will not be so bad if you have a good reason for having all this extra stuff, for instance if you are storing it for someone else. If you are intending to downsize, then you will not have room for this clutter in your new home, so you will need to get rid of it anyway.

1.8 People who can help you declutter, charities and sale of goods.

There are local companies which will come round and clear your house or room etc for you either for free or inexpensively. Your local paper should have details or you can look online.

There are other companies which will come and help you to organise things and use the storage in your house more efficiently.

Councils will usually come and collect a certain number of large items from outside your house or the ground floor for a small sum. In Westminster it is £22 for 5 items, plus a little extra for each extra large item. You can ring your local council to find out how to arrange and book this service.

People often sell their unwanted items on sites like Ebay or Gumtree nowadays, although if the income which could be generated in this way is not worth the effort, consider instead giving the items to a charity. It is quicker and simpler to give the items to charity or throw them away than to try to sell them, although sometimes it is easier to get rid of a large item through selling it for a pittance on Ebay rather than try to handle it yourself. I prefer to give things to charity as the things I give away are not things that I miss and if I do not have a use for it, then I would prefer that someone in need does.

Some charities will come to your home to collect large items or lots of items.

You can put things into storage, but my experience is that storage can be just an expensive way of holding the rubbish that you do not need and really will never use again. (Don't forget that storage companies usually also charge a compulsory insurance which significantly increases the cost). You can hire a self-storage place or get removal men to put things into storage for you.

1.9 Make the time to declutter

In order to declutter, you may have to go through each room, shelf by shelf, a bit each day or you may be able to blitz it in a day. It depends on how you like to work. Either

**The Expert's Guide on How to Sell a House in the UK:
helping you to sell well.
by Dr Judith Summer.**

---

way, schedule time to do this, and do not put it off. Book an appointment with yourself. It is just as important as booking a slot at the hairdresser or booking to have drinks with your friends.

1.10 Summary top tips

I cannot stress enough how much better a property looks once it has been de-cluttered. And therefore how much easier it is to sell. A home can looked lived in and comfortable as well as neat and uncluttered!

The Expert's Guide on How to Sell a House in the UK:
helping you to sell well.
by Dr Judith Summer.

Chapter 2

Floors, furnishings and smells

2.1   Wood floors

2.2   Rugs and carpets

2.3   Flowery, lacy or frilly soft furnishings

2.4   Colours

2.5   Beds

2.6   Curtains

2.7   Dressing the property for sale

2.8   Smells

2.9   Summary top tips

When preparing your house for sale, you may need to take a step back to see what your floors and soft furnishings etc would look like to a potential buyer. What impression is your home giving? What market are you aiming at? Will the internal decor of your house attract the market you are aiming at?

2.1   Wood floors

If you have a beautiful wood floor, even one with a few marks and scratches, it would be best to show it off. Wood floors are popular and really help to sell a property, but there is no point hiding them under huge rugs, unless the floor is in really bad

condition. If that is so, you could consider getting it re-sanded, but this costs a lot, should be done by a professional and is messy so it is up to you, and it may be better to keep a large rug in place. A smaller rug is fine on a wood floor as it should still allow the floor to be shown off.

2.2 Rugs and carpets

If you have an old fashioned or traditional rug, and it is not plain, please consider rolling it up and putting it away, even if at some point it was a really expensive rug. Even if it still is a really expensive rug. You want people viewing the property to see the size of the room, and not get hung up on the threadbare rug in the middle of the room, or the big flowery one with the terrible matching flower cushions. I really hate traditional Persian rugs, and I am sure that I am not the only one who views them as old fashioned, even in a traditional sort of property. If in doubt about a removing a rug, maybe ask your estate agent to give his honest opinion.

Rugs in kitchens should probably be removed too as that is not where people expect them to be, and it only highlights that the kitchen floor is hard and cold. Maybe leave a small rug near the kitchen sink if that is where it lives, and leaving a small one by the back door should be fine.

If, however, your carpet is old-fashioned or very bright, you could consider either replacing it throughout (an expensive option, and may not be necessary) or covering it with a large, plain rug.

2.3 Flowery, lacy or frilly soft furnishings

Flowery, lacy, frilly things in general give an old fashioned air and should be removed if they are everywhere. One thing or set of things like one or two cushions should not matter, but a whole living room full of them will give a different impression to the room. Lace doilies on side tables are not necessary and look terribly fussy and old-fashioned. Instead put plant pots in appropriate drip trays and use coasters when needed. You can buy inexpensive, plain cushion covers to put over the cushions you have. If the armchairs and sofas are very patterned, you should consider covering them with a throw. Shops like Ikea sell inexpensive ones. The idea is to streamline

The Expert's Guide on How to Sell a House in the UK: helping you to sell well.
by Dr Judith Summer.

---

everything into a plain, neutral and inoffensive state. Even if you are marketing your home to the older generation, a neutral set of furnishings cannot offend. You do not want anyone's eye to be drawn to the sofa instead of the size of the room.

2.4   Colours

The more coloured your room is, the more neutral you need to make the furnishings. Only if your room is already neutral can you add a splash of colour with the furnishings, and only a small splash. You do not want to put off people who do not like the colour with which you choose to splash. Plain white tablecloths are good if you need a tablecloth.

2.5   Beds

Cover beds, especially unused beds with a plain white bedspread or simply a plain white sheet. If you do not have white, but something that is plain and neutral, that is also fine. This is not so important in a room that is clearly a child's room. A neutral duvet cover with one coloured throw and matching pillows/ cushions is a nice touch.

2.6   Curtains

If you have big flowery curtains and drapery in living rooms you could consider removing them and leaving just the net or roller blind. This will let much more light into the room and again the eye will not be drawn to the big, overpowering pattern which may not be to the viewer's taste. If the rest of the room is decluttered and frill free, then this may not be such an issue though as long as the curtains are left open, even on a night viewing.

2.7   Dressing the property for sale

If your property is empty and especially if it is in a prime area, you may have to dress it for sale, especially if no buyers are biting when the property is empty. By this I

**The Expert's Guide on How to Sell a House in the UK:
helping you to sell well.
by Dr Judith Summer.**

mean that you may have to install things like furniture, paintings, mirrors, soft furnishings, books, vases, soap and towels etc, so that the property feels lived in, in a kind of dream catalogue kind of way. The buyers can then understand what all the different spaces are for and imagine themselves inside their dream home. There are companies which will dress a property for you, but the fees can be quite high, with a set up fee followed by a monthly fee, and the costs add up if your property is on the market for a long time, even if August and December are offered for free. An alternative is buying the furniture etc yourself, perhaps with the help of a designer, and then afterwards selling it, giving it away or using it yourself. However, in a strong market, dressing a property almost always gets a rapid response, unless the property is overpriced or something else is obviously wrong.

2.8 Smells

People respond positively to good smells, and a home should smell nice at all times. It will give a subtly good impression, even if there is not bad smell to mask. If there is a bad smell, you need to need the cause and check it is nothing that needs addressing, like a damp smell from a leaking pipe. I nearly did not buy the house my family lived in for a decade, because on the viewing there was a damp smell which an overpowering burning joss stick did not quite hide and it gave an overwhelmingly negative impression of the house.

I like using diffusers, but not the cheap nasty ones which you can get from supermarkets. A cheap nasty smell will make your home seem cheap and nasty, and they are often overpoweringly sickly. That will not help you sell your house. You can also spend huge amounts of money on diffusers which is not necessary. I suggest buying middle of the range ones from department stores, and having one in any ground floor WC, the main living area and the master bedroom. If you are selling a smaller place you may not need as many.

2.9 Summary top tips

It is important to work out who the main market for your home is, ie what sort of people are likely to want to buy your property. You need to imagine yourself as an outsider from that category of people and try to see what they will see and whether

**The Expert's Guide on How to Sell a House in the UK:
helping you to sell well.
by Dr Judith Summer.**

---

your furnishings will match what they want. Your estate agent will be able to help you with setting your target market and should be able to give you an objective overview of how your furnishings come across. Do not get offended at the thought that they may not like your taste. This is business, not personal.

The Expert's Guide on How to Sell a House in the UK:
helping you to sell well.
by Dr Judith Summer.

Chapter 3

Repairs and renovations

3.1 Repairs

3.2 Painting

3.3 When a property clearly needs renovation

3.4 Summary top tips

When preparing a home for sale, the question often arises as to how much renovation and repair work is necessary. So many popular renovation TV programmes are running that it seems like everyone has to turn into a professional developer to sell their home. This is not the case. If in doubt, ask what the estate agent or agents selling your home for you think.

3.1 Repairs

Whilst I am not suggesting you have to refurbish your whole house in order to sell it, you should repair anything which is glaringly wrong or broken. Is there a dripping tap, toilet or gutter? The viewer or their surveyor will notice these little things, and there is no point putting them off before you start if an inexpensive repair can be effected in a short period of time. You don't want a prospective buyer not making an offer because he thinks that there must be other more serious issues wrong with the property if even the glaring ones are not fixed.

Small and easy fixes are the idea here. If there is a hole in the carpet, it may not be necessary to replace the whole carpet, but perhaps a plain rug would be a good idea. If there are bulbs which have blown it is worth replacing them.

3.2 Painting

How many times have you heard people talk about putting on a lick of paint to help sell a house? It is true that a newly painted property, painted in light, neutral shades will probably make an advantageous difference, in the UK at least, as the property will look bright and fresh. The same may not be true outside of the UK; I am told that Italians approach a newly painted house with suspicion, wondering what is hidden underneath!

But let us assume that where you are selling, UK attitudes prevail. Painting the whole house may be costly and impractical, and you may be able to get away with painting only the halls and stairways. Even if the paintwork in most of a property looks fine, the stairway and hall can look grubby with finger marks up the wall, so it may well be worth getting at least this area of the house re-painted. A handy tip: baby wipes are amazing for cleaning paintwork and walls, although be careful because they also wash some of the wall paint away. If your property was newly painted recently, you may not need to re-paint at all.

If the common parts of a block of flats or conversion need re-painting, that can be quite a turn-off as the viewer is given a bad first impression. So if you can persuade the management to repaint the common parts, or even just get it done yourself, you will be in a better position.

3.3 When a property clearly needs renovation

Sometimes properties have not been updated for many years, look very old-fashioned and may be in quite a bad state. It is not necessarily the case that you should renovate a property like this before sale. There are a number of buyers who want to come in and make their own stamp on a place, and your property will be attractive to them because they will be able to do this. They may well have been looking for this sort of opportunity for a while. So if you try to make everything as decluttered, neutral and plain as you can, that is all you probably need to do. You probably would not even need to paint a property like this.

**The Expert's Guide on How to Sell a House in the UK:
helping you to sell well.
by Dr Judith Summer.**

I recently saw a house for sale which had not been touched in some 50 years. The estate agent advised the seller that because water stains on the ceiling were clearly very old, it was obvious that there was not a big roof issue and as the whole house needed renovation, it was not even necessary to paint over the old water stains. He was right, as the house sold very quickly and above the expected level. But it had been decluttered and neutralised as per my consultation.

Remember, often properties which need refurbishment are priced so that if you add in the cost of the development, there is no profit. The seller might be wiser to price the property very carefully, bearing in mind a quotation for the cost of the works, rather than try to carry out the works himself. In fact, the seller might even do better in this scenario than doing the work himself, as people tend to underestimate the amount it will cost to do the work, and so overestimate how much they can pay to buy the property in the first place.

Speak to your local estate agent if you wish to do a full refurbishment yourself. It may be that the cost of that refurbishment will equate to the extra amount that you might be able to sell your home for, so would not be worth it. Seasoned developers make their money by buying at a discount, before they have even picked up a hammer. It also takes a certain amount of skill and know-how to be able to refurbish a property to a level which makes it worth more than the cost of the refurbishment, and it usually involves increasing the square footage of the property or adding value in some other way depending on the exact circumstances of the property.

Ways of adding value in some other way include redistributing the space so that wasted space is used; installing an en suite in the master bedroom; putting in a ground floor WC; and/or modernising the wiring, plumbing and decor. It usually also involves a finish to an impressive standard especially in prime property areas if the seller is going to achieve top money, because the market for a fully refurbished property usually wants to walk into a ready made home where they do not have to touch a thing and they want to be impressed. Other "done up" properties they may be viewing may have the wow factor with which your "done up" property will have to compete. Depending on your area, you may need to add extras like fancy electrics, and also dress the place for sale.

Remember, if you are doing up your home, you may need to move out, so the budget for the refurbishment needs to include accommodation costs. Projects with people still

Simma Properties - Finding your little property treasure
Copyright © 2016 Judith Penina Summer
All rights reserved.

The Expert's Guide on How to Sell a House in the UK: helping you to sell well.
by Dr Judith Summer.

---

living in the property tend to take longer than projects without people or furniture in the way.

3.4 Summary top tips

You should fix any obvious problems and consider whether your property could do with some painting, and if so how much. Unless you particularly want to renovate a run-down property yourself, it may not be worth doing it, but you should liaise carefully with your estate agent to get the pricing of the sale right. It would be worth you getting an estimate for doing the work so that you can get the sale price right.

**The Expert's Guide on How to Sell a House in the UK:
helping you to sell well.
by Dr Judith Summer.**

Chapter 4

Preparing the outside for sale

4.1   Front and back gardens

4.2   Big trees and overhanging foliage

4.3   Fences

4.4   Bins

4.5   Front door

4.6   Window frames and sills

4.7   Guttering and hoppers

4.8   Summary top tips

When preparing a property for sale, the outside space will be just as important to consider as the inside. In fact, the front of a property will probably be even more important as this is what every potential buyer will see on every first approach to the building. First impressions make the most difference, just like with an interview. I know of an example where the viewer literally would not get out of the estate agent's car to look at the stunning inside of a newly refurbished house because the outside of the neighbour's house, and not even the house for sale, was in a decrepit state. Here follow some things to consider beautifying.

**The Expert's Guide on How to Sell a House in the UK:
helping you to sell well.
by Dr Judith Summer.**

4.1 Front and back gardens

Any lawn must be mowed with leaves raked, beds weeded and plants and hedges clipped neatly so nothing is overhanging on to a lawn or pathway. Anything overhanging will make the space seem smaller. Driveways, patios and pathways should be swept and weed free. You should also clear your gardens of any rubbish - old tyres and bicycles that do not work are not attractive! Bulbs are an inexpensive way to brighten up a flowerbed. If you know you would like to put your house on the market in the spring, plant bulbs in advance in the autumn. Some plants in pots either side of a patio or patio door can make the area brighter as long as you remember to water them.

A garden, front or back, can be neatened in just a day, and this makes so much difference. If this is work you cannot do yourself, consider hiring a gardener both for the once off job of tidying the garden up and for the job of maintaining it until a sale. In winter, very little maintenance is needed. In spring and summer, the maintenance might be once a week or you might get away with once a fortnight.

4.2 Big trees and overhanging foliage

If you have trees in the front or the back of your house that are overbearing then they may need pruning, and you may have to hire professionals to do this. If you are in a conservation area or the tree is protected by a TPO (a tree preservation order), you will need to get planning permission from the council first. Overbearing trees can darken rooms and shadow huge patches of garden, so getting them pruned is really important as it will make a dramatic difference to the light to your property, and light is one of the most important influencers.

You should also cut back foliage which is overhanging from a next door property into yours. You are entitled to do this, but I leave it to your discretion as to whether you wish to talk to your neighbour before you go ahead. It will depend on your relationship with them. Bear in mind the need for permission from the council if you are in a conservation area or if the tree in question is protected.

4.3 Fences

Wooden fences should be mended if broken, and varnished. Nothing should look dilapidated. Consider dealing with a fence even if it is not your responsibility, but try to speak with your neighbour as you may be able to come to an arrangement with them, perhaps sharing the cost, or perhaps they will pay for it if you arrange the work. If you deal with the fence, even if you have to pay for the whole thing, you will benefit even if it is the neighbour's fence.

4.4 Bins

Is there any way that you can screen off unsightly bins, perhaps with some plants or plant pots, or put them in a bin store? Bin stores can be made or bought inexpensively, but you may need planning permission to build them, especially if you live in a conservation area. You may decide to take the view to go ahead regardless, on the basis that you only want a bin store in the short term and that you will have sold your house by the time anyone complains! The key is to make any bin store not too big and in good taste. A good way to do this is to paint or varnish it the same colour as the wall or fence on which it will lean.

4.5 Front door

It makes a very bad impression if a front door has peeling paint or varnish, and this is something that really should be addressed, unless perhaps you are selling a dilapidated wreck, in which case the front door will be renewed or replaced by the new owner anyway. Polish up any door furniture like letter boxes and knockers and clean the door, especially any glass on the door. Wipe away cobwebs formed on the underside of the porch. Clean any front door step. A new, plain, outside mat would be an attractive addition.

There are extreme examples where the front door needs to be replaced to attract buyers. I saw a really expensive multi-million pound house recently which was not selling. I am sure the reason is that it did not look attractive from the outside where the double front door was a large and prominent eyesore. This property needed an

ultra modern silver metal and glass front door to match both the interior and exterior decor, rather than its old-fashioned glass and white metal bars design. The front door made the property look like it belonged to a council estate rather than to the exclusive area in which it resided.

An instant wow factor can be achieved if you put a freestanding potted plant by the front door, or even better if there is room, a matching potted plant either side of the front door. Small, neat and evergreen is the key. These plants can be inexpensive and can be moved with you to your new home. Look in your local DIY store for box plants, which commonly come in spiral, ball or cone shapes. A more expensive option would be the lollipop shape (called a standard) in perhaps boxus or Red Robin. Choose the shape and plant you like that matches the space you have with a plain sort of pot probably in black or grey.

You can add small bedding plants if you want. For the non-gardeners amongst us, these are small flowering plants that die at the end of a season but look very attractive whilst in bloom. Pansies are common through the winter months, and geraniums through the summer months, but there are many more.

Make sure the plants and pots are watered during the summer! Remember that hanging baskets need a lot of watering so do not get one if that is not the sort of thing you are likely to do on a daily basis.

4.6 Window frames and sills

Unless you are selling a wreck, the house should not look like a wreck on the outside. The impression that the windows make is important too. The windows, frames and sills should be clean. If you have wooden frames and sills, consider painting them. This will be more important if they are obviously flaking.

4.7 Guttering and hoppers

Guttering and hoppers (the top of the drainpipe that catches the water from the roof) should usually be cleared of leaves at least twice a year, perhaps before and after autumn. Make sure this has been done, as firstly it will look better if it can be seen

The Expert's Guide on How to Sell a House in the UK: helping you to sell well.
by Dr Judith Summer.

---

from the road, and secondly blocked guttering and hoppers is a common source of leakage into a home. When you are trying to sell you home, the last thing you need is a wet patch appearing in the inside of your beautifully decluttered and re-painted house.

4.8 Summary top tips

First impressions count, and so getting the front of your house to look attractive is time and effort worth spent. Neat and tidy with the property showing no obvious problems is the key here. Obviously, if you are selling your property as a wreck to be done up, you do not need to do so much work to the front of the place, although it would still pay to keep it weeded and neat.

The Expert's Guide on How to Sell a House in the UK:
helping you to sell well.
by Dr Judith Summer.

Chapter 5

Appointing an estate agent

5.1   Do you need an estate agent?

5.2   "Online" estate agents

5.3   The value that an estate agent adds to the process

5.4   What if someone approaches you for a private sale?

5.5   How do you appoint the right estate agent?

5.6   How many estate agents should you appoint

5.7   Summary top tips

5.1   Do you need an estate agent?

I think you are probably better off appointing an estate agent, even though it is you, the seller, who will have to pay his sales commission upon completion of a sale. I have never seen an example where someone got a better price for their sale by not going through an estate agent, even taking into account the saved estate agent costs

I know that people advertise their properties privately in the local paper and via social media instead of appointing an estate agent, and some of them must succeed in achieving a sale. Advertisements are not free, but would usually be cheaper than an estate agent's fees. But I cannot see how an individual can possibly hope to reach the audience that an estate agent can both through an agent's own website and offices and via online search facilities like Primelocation, Rightmove or Zoopla. I have been

watching the same advertisement for a flat being sold by a Mr Private Individual, being repeated in my local paper every week for the last 7 months.

I think buyers expect estate agents to be holding the best properties and tend to be suspicious of sales which are offered without agents.

5.2 "Online" estate agents

Many "online" estate agents are now available, which offer to place your property on the property portals for a fee, usually payable if a sale is achieved, which is usually much less than the fee payable to a non-virtual entity. But an online agent does not do all that an actual estate agent does. I would usually advise that a seller signs up with an actual estate agent, because I value what an estate agent does, especially a good one:

5.3 The value that an estate agent adds to the process

1. *Agents have access to the most buyers.* Buyers tend to go to estate agents in the first instance when they are serious about looking for properties and estate agents are good about knowing which buyers are out there. They might even know about the potential buyer who is not actively looking but would consider moving if the right property came along. It might be your property, and the estate agent is the only one who would know to contact him.

2. *Estate agents can match buyers to sellers and create the moving opportunities.* The best estate agents will not be just a portal exchange but will be more active. So for instance, they might know that X is thinking of selling, and buyer B would love X's house. If only he can persuade X to move. Aha, X would love property Y, so if he shows X property Y, even though X is not set on selling he might sell if he likes property Y. And then, even though X's house is not officially on the market, buyer B might view it and a two sale deal is done.

3. *Estate agents can help you in your related purchase.* Estate agents know which properties are or might be for sale but are not yet on the market, and they might well be able to help you in your purchase too. People do not realise that the very best

**The Expert's Guide on How to Sell a House in the UK:
helping you to sell well.
by Dr Judith Summer.**

---

properties are often snapped up before they even reach an online portal. You want the estate agent to know you, so he can match you to your dream home, which means you will be in a position to sell the house registered with him and he will earn his commission from both the sale of your house and the related purchase of one of his properties.

4. *Advertising.* Estate agents have the widest advertising reach and can place your property on their own websites, all the best property portals, their own office windows and appropriate property magazines. They also know which photographers to instruct to take professional photographs of your property, and are expert at choosing which images should be included in your campaign as being the ones which are most likely to help sell your property.

5. *Advice for optimising a sale.* Estate agents know their local market better than anyone and can advise on optimising a property for sale and also on price. More on price later. If you want to know if a rug should be taken out etc, it is a good idea to ask your estate agent, as he will know how the majority of his local market would view such a rug etc.

6. *Showing a property.* Estate agents know how to show a property. It looks easy and you might be able to do it yourself, but the professional is almost always better and the buyer usually prefers you to be out of the way on a viewing.

7. *Intermediary.* It is very useful to have an intermediary in the negotiation process between you and the buyer. The agent can advise on whether or not you should accept an offer, although if you follow my advice below, you should have a good idea of this yourself.

5.4 What if someone approaches you for a private sale?

Rarely do both the buyers and the sellers know enough to be on an equal footing in a situation where a buyer approaches a seller directly without an estate agent. I have seen a vulnerable seller, a lady living on her own in her 80's, being told that her next door neighbour's friend would like to buy her house. She relaxed and nearly agreed. What a nice man he is...etc etc. If I had not intervened in time, she would have sold to him, as she assumed that the nice man was offering her a good price, and anyway

someone else down the road sold at that sort of price. In the end she got £75,000 more through an estate agent. On a house worth less than £500,000 that is a large proportion. 15% different.

If someone approaches you and wants to sell without the estate agent, especially if one is engaged, you should be suspicious. I would advise that you tell your estate agent immediately and let the process go through the agent in the normal way. This sort of buyer usually wants to buy the property cheaply and hopes you might agree his offer without consulting the agent. He might argue that the property should be cheaper if you are not going to have to pay the agent's commission, or he might ask to split the difference between what the property would cost with and without a commission. It is true that if the agent does not source the buyer, you do not have to pay the agent's commission. However, this will be subject to the argument that the buyer only knows about the property because of the money and effort that the agent has spent on advertising, and it is likely that the agent will argue for payment of his full commission unless it is clear that the buyer is someone you know or you declared that you had a potential buyer even before the agent was appointed.

If you are approached and you have not appointed an agent, you need to be sure of your property valuation before you agree to a sale. Even at this point you could do some of your own research and ask three agents to give you a free valuation (see further below). You do not have to appoint them.

5.5 How do you appoint the right estate agent?

In order to appoint an estate agent you need to know two things: firstly the value of your property and secondly which are the most active agents in the area. Why do you need to know the value of your property at this stage? Because how can you decide which agent to appoint when you do not know whether or not he is talking rubbish when it comes to the valuation?

As you are going to be relying on your agent to some degree, perhaps you do not need to be so thorough in your valuation research as you do for buying a property. You should look at online sites such as Rightmove or Primelocation for properties equivalent to yours, to see both what they are being offered for (your competition) and what they have sold for in the last 18/24 months or so. If you already know the

total square footage of your home you can work out what the price per square foot of your home should be based on what the price per square foot is on the equivalent sold and for sale properties. However, if you do not know, you may have to wait until an agent has been appointed and a plan has been drawn up before you find out exactly how big your property is.

Whether or not you do your own online research as to value, you should get property valuations from 2 or preferably 3 estate agents. Do some online searches of properties like yours and see which agents' names are coming up the most frequently. It is important to search for properties equivalent to yours, because different agents may have a reputation for different types of property and their core applicant base may be focused on one type of property.

Then get 2 or 3 suitable agents round to estimate for you. Find out what fee they charge. You can probably negotiate on the fee, but there will probably be a bottom line common through the area. The agent probably will not be interested in incentives like you will give them a bigger fee if they sell at a bigger amount.

Do not just appoint the agent who gives you the highest estimate. If the property does not sell at that amount after the first two weeks or so, he will be advising you to lower your asking price. Besides the amount of the estimate, which agent do you prefer? Perhaps you should appoint the agent whose valuation is most in line with your own estimate. Do not feel pressured into agreeing to appoint the most pushy agent or the one who makes you feel guilty. There is an etiquette that you sell the house through the agent from whom you bought it, but you are not bound by this. It is your property and your money, and you can choose who you want as your estate agent.

5.6 How many estate agents should you appoint?

You also need to decide how many estate agents to appoint. If you have a multi-agent sale (ie lots of agents), it will cost you more in fees and I think it makes you look desperate to sell at any price, although those agents will probably reach all the buyers who are registered with all the agents.

If you have only one sole agent, the fees will be less and he will not be able to reach buyers who have not registered with him, but you need to believe that his expertise

**The Expert's Guide on How to Sell a House in the UK:
helping you to sell well.
by Dr Judith Summer.**

---

and advertising will sell it for you. If your property is not selling, make sure the sole agent is prepared to offer a fee to other agents to show your house. A sole agent will usually make a conveyance go smoother, as there is less chance of gazumping by other agents trying to introduce a new seller, and he will do everything he can to make that sale happen.

You can appoint a joint sole agent ie two agents only. The fees will usually be more than for a sole agent, and less than for multi-agents, but you will have the advantage of the registered buyers with both of them. Of course they may have the same buyer base so that this might not be so much of an advantage. You can apply the expertise of both, and both will be competing for the sale or more importantly to them, the greater part of the commission which the selling agent will earn.

Your agreement with the estate agent or agents will tell you the terms on which you have contracted them to work for you, and you can try to negotiate on these before you sign if you are not happy. For instance, you may not want a sole contract for two months, but only one. The contract does not usually tie you to an agent forever, so make sure you are happy that the contract ties you for as long as you want it to.

5.7 Summary top tips

I would always appoint an estate agent (actual not virtual) and use them for their marketing expertise and to ask them for advice about the state of the property and who the active market in the area are. I would appoint one estate agent or two, but not usually multiple agencies. Remember, they work for you, so if you are not satisfied, you can change after a certain period of time, although your agreement with them will specify the terms and conditions of stopping an instruction. You can and should ask them to keep you informed of viewings and the feedback from each applicant. Always try to work out yourself what the true value of your property is, so you can gauge yourself whether an offer to buy is a good or reasonable one.

The Expert's Guide on How to Sell a House in the UK:
helping you to sell well.
by Dr Judith Summer.

Chapter 6

Preparing your property for a viewing

6.1   Clean and tidy

6.2   Beds

6.3   Flowers

6.4   Garden

6.5   Light

6.6   Temperature

6.7   Pets

6.8   People out of the way

6.9   Smells

6.10 Checklist

6.11 What if you only have half an hour's notice before a viewing?

6.12 Summary top tips

Once you have done the general preparations described above in preparing your home and appointing your agent, you will still need to make sure that your property is prepared to optimum effect at each viewing. How do you do this? You do not want to

**The Expert's Guide on How to Sell a House in the UK:
helping you to sell well.
by Dr Judith Summer.**

---

put someone off at a viewing, especially if you have done some work in preparing your property for sale.

6.1 Clean and tidy

The house needs to be clean and tidy for a viewing, so you need to be on a sort of clean house alert the whole time that your property is on the market. If it is your habit to put things into the sink until you have nothing left to eat off, now is the time to cure that habit! If you do not clean until your in-laws come round usually, now is the time to get into a weekly routine. Breakfast things can no longer wait on the side until the evening. Clothes can no longer be thrown on to the floor until you have time to hang them. And if you do not have a laundry bag or basket, you need to get one quickly, because the floor is not a laundry bag. This is also time to make sure you do not start cluttering up the place again, especially the kitchen, so deal with your post immediately and put things away or throw things away straightaway.

6.2 Beds

Beds should be made, and unused beds covered with a white or neutral bed sheet or bed spread. If you have pillows/ cushions for dressing the bed, this is the time to remember to put them on the bed every day in the morning!

6.3 Flowers

Fresh flowers are a nice touch, but a bit over the top if you have to keep buying new ones. Try flowering orchids instead, but make sure not to over water them. I find once every two weeks is plenty.

6.4 Garden

Make sure the garden is in its prepared state during the time that your property is on the market. This might mean you turn into a weekly gardener or that you hire one, even if it is only to mow the lawn every week, but if that is what you need to do...

Simma Properties - Finding your little property treasure
Copyright © 2016 Judith Penina Summer
All rights reserved.

6.5 Light

You need to maximise the light.

So if a viewing is happening by day, open all the curtains through the whole house. If you are going to work, get into the habit of opening the curtains throughout before you leave, in case the estate agent wants to show your property whilst you are out. If a net or blind is not hiding a bad view from a window, open these too, although consider whether you want these open if the property is going to be unoccupied for a large part of the daytime.

Open all the doors through the house. The viewer standing in the hall should get a lovely view of an endless property, which will seem bigger if the doors are open.

Turn all the lights on unless the sun is streaming in so brightly that there is seriously no need.

If you can arrange for viewings around midday, the light is more likely to be at its maximum. If you have an east facing property, morning viewings would be good too, and afternoon viewings for a west facing property. But lunch time should work for whichever way your property faces.

6.6 Temperature

The property should feel ambient and warm. If the property is unoccupied, you still need to have the heating set to keep the place heated to 15-18 degrees to make it feel warm when people are viewing the property (and also to stop pipes freezing in winter). If it is summer hot, open windows if you can do so without there being a security risk. If you have air conditioning, you can either put it on or make sure that the estate agent knows how to do this.

6.7 Pets

Seeing pets - and I don't mean goldfish - can put a viewer off, especially if there is a smell from the pet and pet things, if they are allergic or asthmatic or if they perceive that the animal may have damaged the house. Use air fresheners - as I said before, I like middle of the range diffusers from department stores. A viewing might be a time for a dog walk. Can your pet temporarily live with someone else during the peak viewing period? If not, do not worry. It is what it is.

6.8 People out of the way

Buyers are usually more comfortable if the owner is not at home at the time of the viewing, so make yourself scarce. Even if you work at home, by all means answer the door to the estate agent, and then leave for half an hour or so. Have a walk or a coffee. Take your phone or your laptop. Do what you need to do to be absent. If you cannot be absent, seclude yourself away into one room. Do not follow the agent and prospective buyer around!

If for some reason the estate agent cannot attend, you may have to show the house to the potential buyer. This is rarely optimum. Try to show each room with a natural enthusiasm saying which bits are your favourites and pointing out useful features like an extra coat cupboard in the hallway. Do not start with the WC which is usually near the front door! Perhaps you should let the viewers wonder round by themselves after you have shown them the basic layout.

6.9 Smells

Weird as it might sound, it is important that your home smells nice. People really do think that the smell of fresh coffee or baking makes the property smell homely. If you have diffusers, turn the sticks so you can smell the perfume. In warmer weather, open the windows so that the air smells of the fresh outside.

**The Expert's Guide on How to Sell a House in the UK:
helping you to sell well.
by Dr Judith Summer.**

6.10   Checklist

It is handy to have a checklist of the things you might need to do when you get the call that someone would like to come round and view the property in the next half hour. Eg Clear kitchen surfaces, make beds, plump cushions, open curtains, open doors and turn on lights. As mentioned above, it is helpful if you make yourself live in a "tidy up straight away" sort of way for the duration of the time that your property is on the market, so you do not go into panic mode when you get that call!

6.11   What if you only have half an hour's notice before a viewing?

You can tell the estate agent at what times or days they may show your property, but the more you limit this, the harder it will be for them to find a buyer for you. But sometimes the agent will ring you on short notice saying that he has someone who is free now and not at another time, and asking you if they can come to the house. You may not have much warning, and it would be silly to refuse to show the house just because the hall has not been hoovered in two weeks and the Cornflakes are still out.

If you have only half an hour's notice, do not panic. If you need longer, see if you can persuade them to come in an hour. In half an hour you should have time to race around and: put the toilet seats down; rinse round any dirty sinks; quick hoover or sweep the main hallway, kitchen and living areas; wipe any dirty marks off the kitchen floor and wipe the kitchen surfaces down; plump the cushions; open the curtains; make the beds; turn the lights on. All the day's clutter needs to be put away or thrown away - mugs from the draining board, post from the hall, newspapers from the weekend, remote controls for the TV. Every surface needs to be in its decluttered state, or as near to it as you can in the time available. Bear in mind that people may open cupboards, so throwing clutter in any old how may not help if it is all going to fall out again and make you look like you do not have adequate storage space.

6.12   Summary top tips

Once your home has been prepared, it needs to be kept neat, clean and decluttered. It would be sensible to do a quick clean and tidy up every day as you may not get much

**The Expert's Guide on How to Sell a House in the UK:
helping you to sell well.
by Dr Judith Summer.**

---

notice before a viewing, and make sure the lawn is mowed and the house or flat is cleaned and hoovered properly at least once a week if it is not already. Make an appointment with yourself to make sure you do this. First impressions really do make a big difference. Many viewers cannot see past mess to appreciate the room's aspect and dimensions. You need to be on a sort of "Red Alert" property sale mode, especially in the first two weeks or so of a property being launched on to the market.

Chapter 7

Preparing for the sale process

7.1   Appoint a solicitor

7.2   Documents

7.3   Removal company

7.4   Mental preparation

7.5   Do you have somewhere to move to?

7.6   Obtaining the local searches

7.7   Summary top tips

It is extremely helpful if you can line up what you need as a seller well in advance, as that will help a sale go through quickly. Remember, a buyer can pull out at any time until contracts are exchanged, and he will have less time or incentive to think twice about things, dump your property and go for another one instead, or just get cold feet, if you have your side of things in order and you are able to push things through quickly.

7.1   Appoint a solicitor

You need to appoint a solicitor. This might be someone you used before when buying the property, but only if you liked him or her. Otherwise, ask around your friends and relatives as they may have used a solicitor they like. The estate agent will be able to

suggest someone too. I would not lose too much sleep about which solicitor you want to appoint if you do not know someone already or cannot get a recommendation. Some solicitors offer a fixed fee. Some will charge by the hour, but will be able to tell you before you commit to them the minimum and maximum that the conveyancing will cost. It is easier to choose a solicitor who is local to where you live or work, as at some point you will have to meet him and you may have to take documents to him. He will want to see some identification from every seller as well, so dig out your passport. Ask him what he requires before you even meet him so you can show him your identification documents at your first meeting which he will probably photocopy for his files.

As a rule of thumb, high street solicitors will charge less than bigger firms of solicitors, and this is more pronounced in a metropolis like London where there are high street, West End and City rates. Sometimes though, you get what you pay for.

7.2 Documents

You should get your documents together ahead of time even before an offer has been made so that you do not suddenly have a mad scramble. Once an offer has been accepted, you should send all your documents to your solicitor in one big bundle. The covering letter should ideally list all the documents you include, and then that provides a record for both you and your solicitor. The solicitor should tell you what is required, but this will include anything that you have which might be of use to the buyer eg:

- Leases;

- Insurance schedule - buildings, not contents! The buyer does not need to see what your moveable contents are insured for, but probably does want to know that your building is insured and insurable. If you are selling a flat, the managing agent should send you a copy of the insurance schedule for the building;

- Building guarantees you might have including FENSA window certificates and any new build certificates which are still in date;

**The Expert's Guide on How to Sell a House in the UK:
helping you to sell well.
by Dr Judith Summer.**

- Electric and gas safety certificates if you have any, which you might if you have recently rented out the property or had work done;

- Management information if you are in a flat or private road, relating to management of the building and common parts and management accounts. Again you may need time to request these from the managing agent;

- EPC certificate (an energy rating certificate). You now have to provide this on a sale, and most agents require one before the property is listed, so you should obtain one as soon as possible. They usually cost less than £100 and your estate agent will know who to appoint to draw one up;

- Any notices served on you by the local council, such as notice of nearby works;

- Deeds of Title. If you own your property outright without a mortgage, you will have your Deeds of Title and the solicitor will need this document;

- Mortgage deeds. (If you have an outstanding mortgage) ;

- Any relevant party wall notices or agreements. You will know if you have any of these, and you will have these only if your neighbours have done any structural work recently.

The solicitor will send you some forms for you to fill out, saying which fittings and fixtures you are selling with the property, and asking set questions about the property. They take a while to get through, but please complete them as soon as possible and send them back to your solicitor. You do not want the sale to be delayed whilst you fill out some forms which you could have filled out well in advance.

Once a sale is agreed, the estate agent will send your solicitor a Memorandum of Sale which sets out the basic agreed details of the sale (including the names of the parties and their solicitors, the amount of the sale and the address of the property).

7.3 Removal company

Unless the property you are selling is empty, you will need to find and eventually book a removal company. You should start to look around to see which company you will want to hire as soon as you can, even if you do not yet have a buyer. It will streamline the process for you and make it a lot less stressful if you have this element of the move sorted out before an offer to buy your property comes in or at least before exchange. Otherwise there will be a horrible rush to sort this out between exchange and completion, ie between the time that you commit to selling your house and the date that you commit at exchange to handing over your keys on completion. If you know who your removal company will be, you can liaise with them before you agree a completion date, so you know that you will not have a problem booking your removal company in time.

Speak to companies recommended to you by friends and family. Search online. Normally you can get a rough quotation by filling out an online form or speaking to them over the telephone to say how many rooms need to be packed up. Often they will then visit your property to assess how much stuff you have to move and will give you a full quotation. Then it is only a question of booking them when you know the completion date. If applicable, don't forget to arrange parking permits for the removal company at both ends of the move once you know your dates.

Always ask the removal company to quote for packing up for you too. It is not always so much more for them to pack for you, and in my opinion is well worth the extra money for the saving in time and stress. They can pack huge houses up in a day or two. It would take you weeks. You can go to work giving them the keys and return home to find the house packed up and ready to go the next morning. Also, especially for established companies, they are usually better than you. They know how to pack china without it breaking because they do it every day. They know to remember to label every box with the room from which it has been taken, and to write whether it is books or bedding etc. If you ask them not to pack any private drawers eg those marked with a post-it note, they won't. Although frankly, they are usually too busy and moving too quickly to notice what your underwear looks like.

When it comes to the day before your property is packed up and ready to move, you need to pack yourself a separate suitcase which needs to stay with you. In it you

should put everything you will need for the next couple of days plus all your valuables including: clothes; shoes; children's PE kit and school bags; children's favourite teddy; alarm clock; overnight toiletries; toilet paper (there is no guarantee that there will be any at the new place); kettle; paper/plastic cups/plates/cutlery; cereal box; biscuits (for both you and the removal men!); scissors (to open packing boxes at the other end), sellotape (to re-seal boxes you have inadvertently opened!), pen, Blu-Tack (to put the children's posters on the walls of their new bedroom before they sleep their first night in the room); cleaning cloths and detergent; jewellery; passports and driving licences. Keep your duvets and sheets separate too if you can, so that you can easily make the beds on the first night after the move.

7.4 Mental preparation

You need to be mentally prepared to sell your property. You may be emotionally attached to a property, even one you have never lived in before. Remember, your home is only your home whilst it is occupied by you and your things. After that it is just bricks and mortar and your own memories. But your memories move with you. Take some photos of your home looking nice. And then move on in your mind.

Bear in mind that children need to be mentally prepared for the move too, whether they are young or old, as they can be more attached than you realise to their home and find the process of moving very scary and unsettling. You need to keep telling them what is going to happen and when, and be as reassuring as you can.

7.5 Do you have somewhere to move to?

Having prepared your home for sale, do you have somewhere lined up to live? Some people choose to sell their home and then rent or live with relatives until they find somewhere else to live. That simplifies the selling process, but leaves you having to move twice, once when you sell your home and then again when you move out of your temporary accommodation into the home you buy. If you cannot find anywhere soon, you may be priced out of the market, and the temporary accommodation costs soon mount. You will also incur two sets of moving costs and maybe storage costs too.

**The Expert's Guide on How to Sell a House in the UK:
helping you to sell well.
by Dr Judith Summer.**

If you are selling and also looking for a place to buy at the same time, you need to focus your efforts on the buying process too. I refer you to my ebook "The Expert's Guide to Buying a House in the UK: helping you to buy a good home and a good property investment."

Are you in a position to accept an offer? I would suggest that you do not accept an offer unless you have somewhere else to go, unless the offer is well above the market price. I know someone who was offered £1m over the market value of their house, so agreed to move into rental accommodation until they found somewhere to move to permanently. For £1million I would have made the same decision. However, they have been in that rented accommodation now for over 2 years as they have not been able to find a replacement.

If someone really likes your house, they may be prepared to wait for it. So they may be prepared to exchange in 4 weeks or so but not complete for 6-9 months which may give you long enough to find somewhere else to live.

If you are in a chain like this, hoping to sell your property at the same time as buying another, and using the proceeds of one to help fund the other, you may have to accept a lower offer on your sale to be able to get the timing right. Subject to still being able to afford the purchase, in the scheme of things it may be more important to get the deal done at both ends rather than quibble over money that, although possibly large when taken out of context, will not actually make a difference to your purchase or your future, and when divided over the 25 years of your new mortgage will amount to a pittance.

7.6   Obtaining the local searches

Normally the buyer's solicitor will request local searches on your property from the local council once his offer has been accepted by you. Sometimes he will wait until his mortgage offer has been given before he incurs this expenditure.

However, it is possible for the seller's solicitor to obtain the local searches in advance and pass them and the cost of them to the buyer's solicitor when there is a buyer. This saves on time, especially if the local authority is taking a long time to process such requests. 6-8 weeks is a long time. Some authorities have a turnover of 48 hours

The Expert's Guide on How to Sell a House in the UK:
helping you to sell well.
by Dr Judith Summer.

---

though. The local searches are usually valid and able to be relied upon for 3 months. The buyer is not obliged to accept these from you. He may wish to carry out the searches anew himself and of course, the searches may be invalid by the time you get a buyer. I would suggest that it is only worth considering obtaining local searches in advance if you know your local authority takes a long time to process them and you are in a hurry, perhaps due to a related sale of your property in the chain.

7.7 Summary top tips

Get your selling professionals - solicitors, removal companies etc - lined up as quickly as you can, and collate all the documents you will need. Do not wait for a first offer before you start to get these things in order. Prepare yourself and your family mentally as well as physically for the move.

The Expert's Guide on How to Sell a House in the UK:
helping you to sell well.
by Dr Judith Summer.

Chapter 8

The Sale Process (for England and Wales)

8.1   Offer, exchange, completion

8.2   Timing between offer acceptance and completion

8.3   Gazumping (a new buyer coming along with a higher offer)

8.4   Lock out agreements

8.5   What if the buyer drops his offer?

8.6   Between exchange and completion

8.7   After completion

8.8   Summary top tips

The conveyancing process in Scotland is different to that in England and Wales. For instances, in England and Wales the buyers sends in his surveyor to see if the property has any defects, but in Scotland the seller is obliged to provide a Home Report pack at his cost, within nine days of marketing a property, which includes a survey and valuation. The Scottish system is not discussed further in this book.

8.1   Offer, exchange, completion

After an offer comes in which the seller accepts, the buyer has to find out all he wants to find out about the property and sort out his mortgage if he needs one before he will be ready to commit to the purchase by exchanging contracts. His solicitor will request

The Expert's Guide on How to Sell a House in the UK: helping you to sell well.
by Dr Judith Summer.

---

local searches from the council and documentation and information about the property from your solicitor. If you have been organised, you will already have these ready to send to your solicitor in a bundle, as discussed above.

The buyer and/or his mortgage company will send a surveyor or surveyors in to your property at an agreed appointment to carry out a valuation and/or to find out if there is anything physically wrong with your property. If there are any questions and queries they will be raised by the buyer's solicitor asking your solicitor, and he will ask you if there is any information he needs from you. Make sure to prioritise dealing with your solicitor's queries, as you do not want to delay matters. Be absolutely truthful. If you do not know an answer, say so, and do not guess. Your solicitor should discuss any matters arising with you.

Your solicitor will send the buyer's solicitor a contract for exchange which commits to the buyer buying your house for a certain amount on a certain day, and that day is called the completion date. Once everyone on the buyer's side is happy with the information they have, a completion date has been agreed and the buyer has received any mortgage offer he needs and transferred the appropriate amount of money, he will be ready for exchange. Usually you (ie all the sellers individually) can authorise your solicitor to sign the documents for exchange on your behalf. Other sums can be negotiated, but usually the buyer provides 10% of the purchase price on exchange. This money stays with the seller's solicitor until completion although this may be used for the exchange monies for an associated purchase that you are making.

Once exchange has occurred, the buyer has to complete the purchase (ie provide the rest of the money) and the seller has to vacate the premises by a time and date agreed and set out in the exchange document. Neither party can pull out at this stage without consequences as set out in the exchange document (although there are some rare exceptions which I have never seen in practice, such as if the seller has made some serious misrepresentations which has induced the buyer to buy the property under false pretences). In terms of process, completion occurs when the seller's solicitor confirms receipt of the completion monies from the buyer's solicitor and you will get a call telling you that the sale has completed and to hand over all the keys.

Sometimes the seller hands the keys to the estate agent. Sometimes the seller hands the keys over to the buyer who is sitting in the road with his removal van waiting for the legal process to take place. Delays can occur if there is a problem with the transfer

Simma Properties - Finding your little property treasure
Copyright © 2016 Judith Penina Summer
All rights reserved.

of the money. In that situation the seller has to decide if he will let the buyer in. Once when I was moving into a property, my solicitor confirmed that the monies had been sent for the purchase, but receipt was delayed by the banking system. The estate agent vouched for me and the seller agreed that I could start the process of unpacking my removal van into the house. But keys were not handed over until the money appeared a lot later that afternoon in the account of the seller's solicitor.

8.2 Timing between offer, acceptance and completion

With all that the buyer needs to do, and especially if he needs a mortgage, it could easily take 4-6 weeks until exchange and a further 2/3 weeks until completion. This can be lengthened or shortened, and a lot depends on whether the buyer needs a mortgage and whether he is in a chain. Be patient, but you also have to make sure that the process is still moving along. Your estate agent should be keeping on top of the process and you should be in regular contact with him so that you know what is happening. For instance, has the buyer been approved for a mortgage? Has the surveyor asked for an appointment? Is the buyer's own sale moving along?

Remember that the estate agent is the seller's agent and he is also the one who can telephone the buyer to find out where the buyer is up to in the process. As long as the buyer's difficulties and delays seem reasonable to you and your estate agent, and he gives you a revised timing that you can live with, then give him some leeway. He might for instance, need 8 weeks before exchange, because the local council have a 6 week wait for providing local searches. It this is true, then it is hardly worth you objecting. Perhaps if there is going to be a longer exchange, a shorter time to completion can be negotiated. If the buyer's delays are because of a problem down the chain, you might have to keep your property actively on the market looking for an alternative buyer.

Some agents get very macho and start talking about a two week exchange or else the property will be offered to someone else. I am never sure if it is the agent or the seller getting macho, but it is rarely worth it. There is no point losing a good buyer at a good price because your agent has set an unrealistic deadline for the buyer. Be sensible.

A good agent will usually have a sixth sense as to whether the sale is going pear-shaped. If an excuse for a delay from the buyer sounds a bit dodgy to you, then it may

**The Expert's Guide on How to Sell a House in the UK:
helping you to sell well.
by Dr Judith Summer.**

---

well be that the sale is falling through and that buyer will not be able to buy your property. Sometimes that happens if he cannot get a mortgage through. Sometimes the mortgage valuer has said that your property is not worth what the buyer has agreed to pay, so will not offer him the mortgage he needs. For the equity on the property will not be enough to support the percentage of the value of the property that he wants to borrow. Sometimes this means that you might have to consider reducing the price either for him or another buyer. Sometimes it means that he was trying to borrow too much of a percentage of the value and other buyers will not have the same problem if they are trying to borrow a lesser percentage of the value.

8.3 Gazumping (a new buyer coming along with a higher offer)

If you have accepted an offer, then you should be prepared to accept that offer, rather than just hoping that another better one might come along. I always say the aim is not to get the best deal in the universe - that aim will drive you crazy - but a deal which is acceptable to you.

If the sale is handled right, gazumping (someone coming along with a higher bid) should not have a chance to happen, and you should be in receipt of the highest bid you are likely to get. This is how I would suggest handling a sale:

Firstly, do not accept an offer until everyone who has asked to see the property has seen it and you have a definite no from all the others, (or no they are not offering any more). Ask the agent to get an answer from each viewer and report back to you. Write their feedback down as they report to you, so you know if there was someone from whom the agent has not had an answer. Do not think that you are being trouble to the estate agent: you, the seller, are paying them - they work for you! The most people who are going to view the property will usually do so in the first two or three weeks. Even if there are multiple agents, it is unlikely that a new applicant will come along shortly if the price is unchanged and you have had everyone's feedback/offers. However, beware one agent trying to persuade you to change to a new buyer introduced by him instead of the buyer introduced by the other agent. Is the new buyer really a better bet, or is the agent just trying to earn the bigger proportion of the sale fee.

**The Expert's Guide on How to Sell a House in the UK:
helping you to sell well.
by Dr Judith Summer.**

If gazumping does occur, do you accept the new offer? That is a matter for your conscience. You are not bound by anything until exchange occurs and you do not incur the estate agent fees until exchange either. I suspect you could try going back to the original buyer to ask for a little more, if not the whole amount more. It would be rare that a new offer was significantly more, so I would not lose a good purchaser, who is showing serious intent for the sake of a few thousand pounds. Include in your calculations your own wasted costs (ie what you have already spent in solicitors' fees in dealing with the first buyer). The new bidder may not be able to go ahead with his bid so you might end up having lost two potential buyers.

If you do accept a gazumping offer, although you are not obliged, it would be good form to offer to pay the expenses incurred so far by the buyer you are rejecting.

8.4   Lock out agreements

Do you take the property off the market if you have accepted an offer? I would say yes, but only if the bidder asks you to (which he probably will) and everyone who has asked to see the property has both seen it and given their feedback and any bids. But only take it off for a short period, say 2 or 3 weeks before reviewing the situation.

Then you will want to see progress from the buyer in the first two weeks - solicitors appointed, searches applied for, a surveyor going in and if there is a mortgage, the mortgage valuer should have gone in or at least be booked to go in. That means that the buyer is serious and is spending his own money so it would probably be OK to keep the property off the market for longer. If the buyer is spending his own money, then this is a good sign for you that he is a serious buyer (although the sale can still fall through if, for instance, he does not get his mortgage or his surveyor spots something serious or his chain collapses). As mentioned above, you can find out from the estate agent what the buyers progress is like, as he can telephone the buyer to find out, and he will know when appointments are booked. Once any mortgage offer has come through and a surveyor has reported, the next bit of progress you should see is enquiries being made by the buyer's solicitor to your solicitor. If the buyer is not making significant progress, I would get the property back on the market immediately.

8.5 What if the buyer drops his offer?

Once exchange has happened, the buyer is committed to buying the property in the state he knows it to be at the price he has agreed, at the date of completion. If he does not, the contract will set out the consequences, which are not good for him!

Sometimes, when you have agreed a price and started incurring solicitors' fees the buyer tries to drop his offer before exchange. You have to decide whether to stick with him or not, and this will depend on the reason for him dropping the offer, whether you have other rejected bidders lined up and for how long your property was on the market.

If the buyer has dropped his offer because he cannot afford it, you may have to accept his reduced offer if there is no-one else available, especially if the property has been on the market for a long while. He might not be able to afford it if he cannot get a mortgage at the bid price because the mortgage valuer has not supported the bid. So if he needs to borrow a certain percentage of the property value, say 75%, he will not get a mortgage if the mortgage valuer says that the property is worth less. If this is the case, be very careful about rejecting his revised offer unless you have other bids lined up in a queue. For if a valuer does not value the property at the bid price, other valuers may feel the same. However, other buyers may not need to borrow as much as say 75% and if they only need to borrow 60% of the value that the mortgage valuer gives to the property you would not need to reduce your selling price.

Sometimes the buyer may try to renegotiate the price once the surveyor has reported due to problems the surveyor has found. You are not entitled to see the surveyor's report but if the buyer wants you to believe him that there are issues with your property, it is in his interests to pass a copy to you. If there is something significantly wrong with the property, like subsidence that no-one knew about before the bid was made, then you should consider dropping the price, as every potential buyer will encounter the same issue, and every surveyor will note it. You may prefer to deal with the issue yourself.

If the offer has been dropped due to niggles from the surveyor's report, then I would suggest standing firm. My view is the buyer can either live with having to deal with the niggles or go to hell! There will always be little things that the survey mentions.

There are always little things wrong with a property. A buyer always needs to budget for the costs of dealing with issues at his new property. Sometimes the things mentioned in the report are not really wrong, but just suggestions of things which would cover the surveyor's legal liability, or suggestions of what to do in the future. If they are only niggles, I think it is unlikely that the buyer will walk, as he will also lose the money spent on the survey. I appreciate that my attitude is gung-ho and risks losing a buyer, but I do not appreciate a try-on, and I do not believe that a buyer will really walk if the issues are just small. It is a risk that I would take. I do not know if you should!

8.6 Between exchange and completion

On the selling side, there is very little you need to do from a process point of view between exchange and completion, except getting the completion documents signed and delivered to your solicitor as per your solicitor's instructions.

From a practical point of view you need to vacate the property if you have not already left it, and confirm the booking with the removal company. As I have mentioned above, it is much simpler if you have arranged in advance which removal company you are using, liaised in advance with them about he moving date and determined who is packing up the property and when .

You need to tell people your change of address, but that does not have to happen before completion, as long as you arrange for your post to be forwarded by the post office. This can be arranged online and there is a small fee. I would suggest the forwarding of mail in all cases for at least one year. That catches the annual renewal letters and annual statements that you get but which you may have forgotten exist until you receive the mail in your new property and see that it has been forwarded.

8.7 After completion

After completion you hand over the keys and pay the estate agent. Sometimes your solicitor will pay the estate agent for you out of the received completion monies, but check with him to find out if he is doing this as you will have to approve the transfer and provide the appropriate details.

**The Expert's Guide on How to Sell a House in the UK:
helping you to sell well.
by Dr Judith Summer.**

You should tell your utility companies that you have moved and give them the final readings of your meters on the date of completion so they can give you final bills. Take a photograph of the meters with the final readings on. If you cannot be there at completion, ask your estate agent to do this for you. You will also need to notify your local authority (council tax) and telephone/ broadband provider. Be warned: it always seems to take forever to deal with the utility and telephone companies and the local authority!

8.8   Summary top tips

The system in England and Wales does not commit the buyer (or you!) until contracts have been exchanged, at which time the buyer promises to buy your property and send you (via your solicitor) the rest of the purchase monies at the completion date. The time between the offer and the exchange can be the most stressful. You can minimise this stress by being calm and reasonable. Take advice from your solicitor as necessary. If it is handled correctly, you should not have to deal with gazumping. If there are some unreasonable or strange delays on the part of the seller, you must try to push the process through via the agent and your solicitor. However, don't keep a blind faith that all is well. If you feel that it is not going as it should, the likelihood is that the sale is not going through, which means you may need to remarket the property. If that is the case, it is not the end of the world, even if it means you miss out on a purchase because you are in a chain. It is annoying and upsetting etc, but it is not the end of the world.

The Expert's Guide on How to Sell a House in the UK:
helping you to sell well.
by Dr Judith Summer.

Epilogue

I thought I would conclude with a couple of my mantras:

1.   You do not have to get the best deal in the universe, just the deal that is good for you and works for you.

2.   Property is just bricks and mortar - if you lose out on a sale or purchase, it is not the end of the world and no-one has died. Keep things in perspective.

Good luck on your property journey! :)

Please contact me if you think I can help you further via:

http://www.simmaproperties.co.uk

www.ingramcontent.com/pod-product-compliance
Lightning Source LLC
Chambersburg PA
CBHW061221180526
45170CB00003B/1101